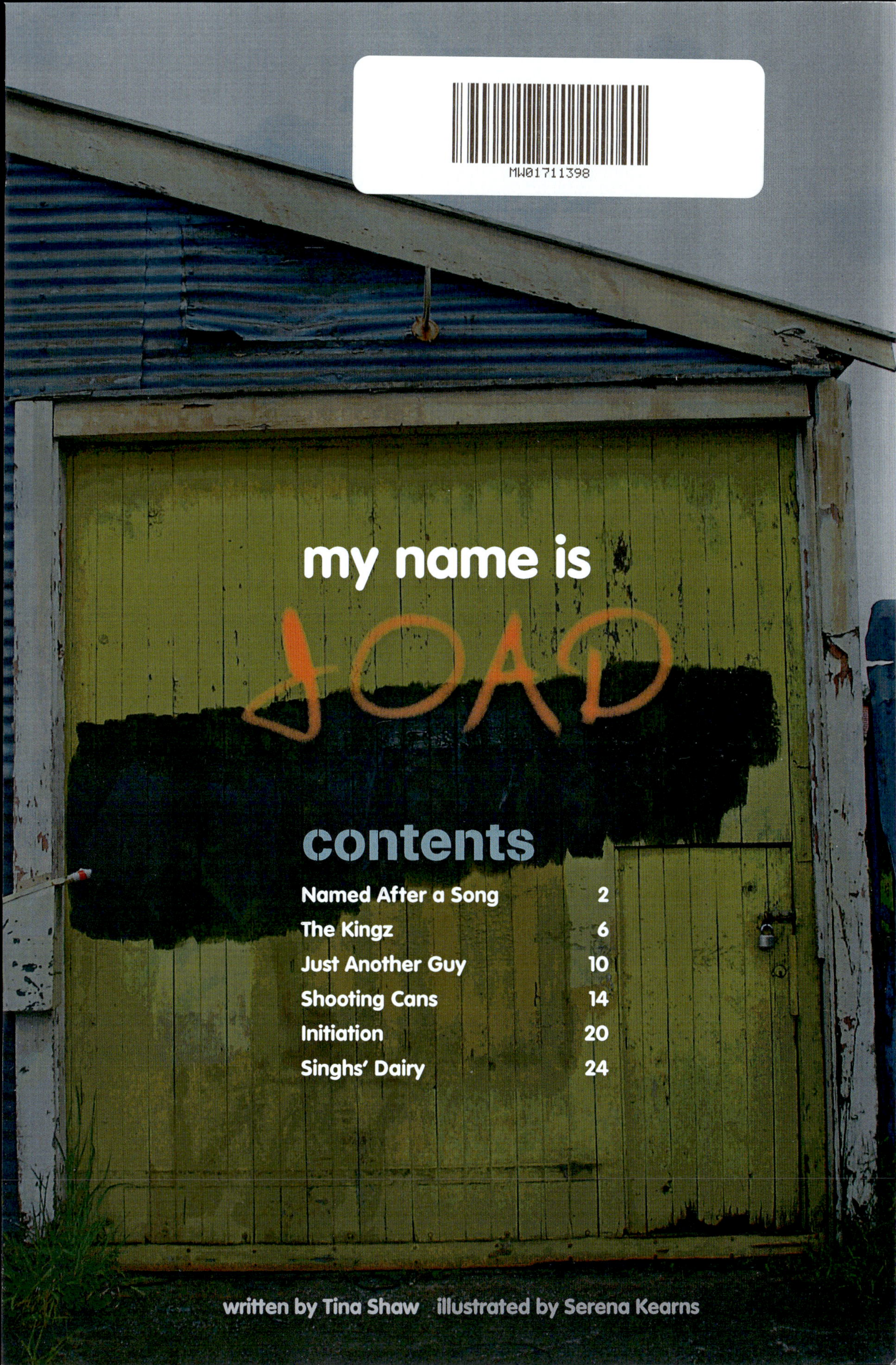

my name is JOAD

contents

written by Tina Shaw illustrated by Serena Kearns

visual features:
How do the visual images and design set the context for the story? What feelings do they evoke?

NAMED AFTER A SONG

My name is Joad. My father gave me my name. Named me after a song, but that's all he did. He took off before I was even born. Ma says he was some big hotshot when he was young, way back when. At least, he liked to think he was. Maybe one day he'll walk back into our lives, and then I can tell him what I really think. If he was such a big hotshot, then why'd he have to leave?

That's what I'm thinking as I go along the towpath beside the river. There's a guy I'm going to meet, down by the bridge. If it goes all right, then maybe he'll let me join the Kingz. It's all I've ever wanted since I was a kid. But they don't take kids in the gang; you've gotta be at least fifteen, and that's the youngest. Even then, you've got to pass the test. You've got to prove yourself. Not just anybody can be in the Kingz. You see these guys hanging round my neighbourhood. They always look so cool – like they know something special. Like they belong.

join the Kingz... it's all I've ever wanted

predict:
Analyse the cover design and illustration and make a prediction about the target audience.

opinion:

"The Kingz don't feel fear. The Kingz only act." **Do you think Joad is gullible for believing this? Why/why not?**

The bridge is up ahead, rising out of the gloom. There's a fire burning in a metal drum, and two guys are warming their hands above the flames. Light flickers orange in their faces. Dark shapes are huddled underneath the bridge. I feel a worm of fear. If anything goes wrong, then it's just me against all of them.

But I'm not gonna show I'm scared. The Kingz don't feel fear. The Kingz only act.

The guys at the fire hear my boots on the gravel. They don't move, just stare.

I keep walking, real steady, till I can see the flames inside the drum and smell the old cardboard and scraps they're burning. Then I stop.

"Whatcha want, kid?"

My throat's dry as sand. "Nelson said to come."

clarify: hotshot, worm of fear

reading between the lines:

What do you think makes Joad receptive (or open) to becoming a gang member?

The two guys shuffle their feet and glance around. One of them lights a cigarette, cupping his hand close to his face. From under the bridge, three more guys appear. The tall one, that's Nelson.

He walks straight over to me while the others hang back and holds out his hand. We slap palms, then he puts a grip on my knuckles. He's crushing my fingers, but I hold his stare.

It could go either way. Could end up being real bad for me. But I want to show him that I'm tough enough to be in the Kingz, so I hold his stare.

Then Nelson nods and lets go. "So you wanna join the Kingz."

"Yeah," I say. "True." I'd been pestering him for weeks. Hanging close, though not too close; following him around. Sometimes I'd just stand on a corner, waiting for Nelson to see me, to make a sign. Yesterday, at the skate bowl, he sent one of his guys over with a message: Nelson wanted to talk, and he told me where to go.

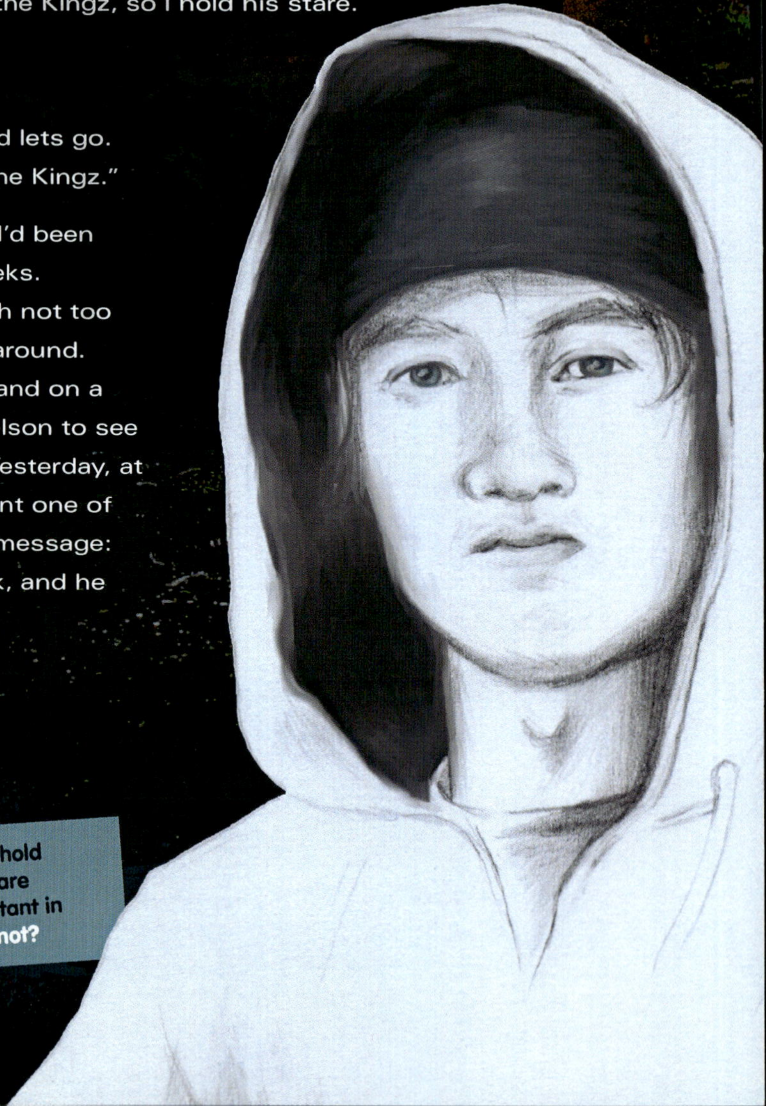

beyond the text:

Why does Joad feel that he must hold Nelson's stare when his knuckles are crushed? Is body language important in projecting toughness? Why/why not?

personal response:
What feelings are evoked in you when Joad says he will do whatever it takes to join the Kingz?

clarify: big time

"Why should I take you on?"

"Cause I'm tough enough."

"How much d'you wanna be in the Kingz?" asks Nelson, orange light shining on his smooth head. Behind him, the other guys are silent, watching.

"Big time," I say.

"What would ya do to join the Kingz?" He squints at me, as if wondering what I'm made of.

It's not something I need to think about. "Whatever it takes."

research:
Research body language and how it communicates feelings.

...I'm tough enough

THE KINGZ

My father was in a gang when he was around my age. That's how he and Ma first met. She was working in a picture theatre when his gang came in and sat up the back. They started acting up – throwing popcorn and laughing real loud at the movie. People were leaving the theatre, too scared to say anything in case they got beat up.

But Ma marched right up there to the back row and shone her torch in their faces. "You dorks better behave," she hissed, "or I'll call the cops."

It cracks me up when she tells that story. But Ma is staunch, so I reckon it's true.

language feature:

Simile/Metaphor/Personification/Colloquialism

What literary device has the author used here? What was the purpose for using this device? How did it help your understanding of the situation?

clarify: staunch

issue: What issues surround the formation of gangs in society? Should gangs be banned? What is your stance on this?

You don't act up when Ma's around, simple as that. If she knew I was meeting Nelson, she'd have a fit. She says if it wasn't for that gang my father was running with back then, he'd never have taken off. She says my father became a different person when he was with his gang. She hates gangs like a snake hates a mongoose.

beyond the text:

What connections can you make to the fact that Joad is hiding his meeting with Nelson from his mum?

setting:

Is Joad being unwise meeting with the Kingz in this setting? Why/why not? What elements in the setting do you think represent danger?

"Let's take a walk," says Nelson.

We leave the bridge behind and walk along the towpath. It's dark, but every now and then a streetlight shows the way. Our boots sound loud on the gravel, and the water on our right is oily black. I try not to think about how I could end up in that stinking river, and Ma would never see me again. Kids tell stories about the Kingz – about how they vanish people they don't like. Snuff you out like a candle.

There was a guy a while back, his body turned up in the river. Maybe he'd got on the wrong side of somebody. People say it was the Kingz who did it.

language feature:

SYMBOLISM

What symbolism did the author use here? How did it help your understanding? What did the author want to convey to the reader?

question:

What strategies are used by Nelson to sell gang membership to Joad?

In the dark space between two streetlights, Nelson stops and lights a cigarette. His eyes are black when he looks at me. "Here's the deal," he says. "Not just anybody can be in the Kingz."

This is the moment I've been waiting for. He is going to set me the test. I hold my breath and shove my hands in my jacket pockets so Nelson won't see them shaking. I'm scared about the test, though I'd never show it. Whatever Nelson tells me to do, I'll do it. I may be skinny, but I can be tough, just like the Kingz.

"We've got this..." He smiles then – a thin smile. "This initiation." Smoke coils around his head.

"I've heard," I say.

...snuff you out like a candle

"It's different for everybody," says Nelson. "Not everybody can do it. That's how we know if you're any good – if you're tough enough to be in the Kingz. Sorts out the sheep from the Kingz," he says with a chuckle.

Me, I don't dare laugh at his cheap joke. Just wait, holding my breath, mouth dry as dust. He drops his butt on the ground and crushes it out with his boot. The river is silent and eerie. Nelson fixes me with a look.

"Here's what you're gonna do..."

clarify: snuff you out, initiation, eerie

issue: What is your stance on the ethics of cigarette companies in promoting the image that smoking is tough? Research the effects of smoking on health and the issues that arise.

JUST ANOTHER GUY

When I was a kid, I used to nag Ma to tell me about my father and his gang, but she hates talking about that stuff. "He was no hero," was all she'd say, giving me a funny look.

As I walk back along the towpath, back to River Road, I'm wondering what initiation my father would have done to join his gang. There would've been something. One way or another, you've gotta prove yourself. Maybe he had to smash one of the big windows at the church. Maybe he had to tag the blue-walled police station down the road. Maybe he had to set a fire at the local school. He would've been tough, my father, 'cause he was in that gang.

Right now, with Nelson's words ringing in my ears, I really want to ask him:

"What would you do if you were in my shoes?"

I come out on River Road and go past the rundown houses with their broken fences and overgrown yards. Past the pub on the corner, music banging out into the night. Turning into Kelvie Street, I scuff along, hands in my pockets.

My heart feels like stone.

Maybe it would've been better if Nelson had thrown me in that stinking river.

personal response:

What feelings are evoked by the author's description of Joad's distress as he thinks about the initiation test?

plot:

Why does the author not reveal what the initiation test is at this point? What do you think will happen in the plot now?

...my heart feels like stone

I've wanted to be in the Kingz for ages – watching Nelson for months, willing him to see me, wanting to talk to the man, watching out for his gleaming chopper down at the mall. It felt so good, the first time Nelson talked to me. "What's ya name, kid?"

Up close, he wasn't that old – more like an older brother.

One time, I saw him with Ms Trent from school. She was tiny, my art teacher. I hadn't realised before how small she was, until I saw her pushed against a wall, with Nelson plucking the DVDs out of her hands like they were flies. I laughed then, to see him skim the DVDs across the car park.

setting:
What inferences can you make about Joad's community from the setting? Are your views affected by social prejudice?

opinion:
Do you think Joad should have taken some action when Nelson bullied Ms Trent? **Why/why not?** What would you have done in the same circumstances?

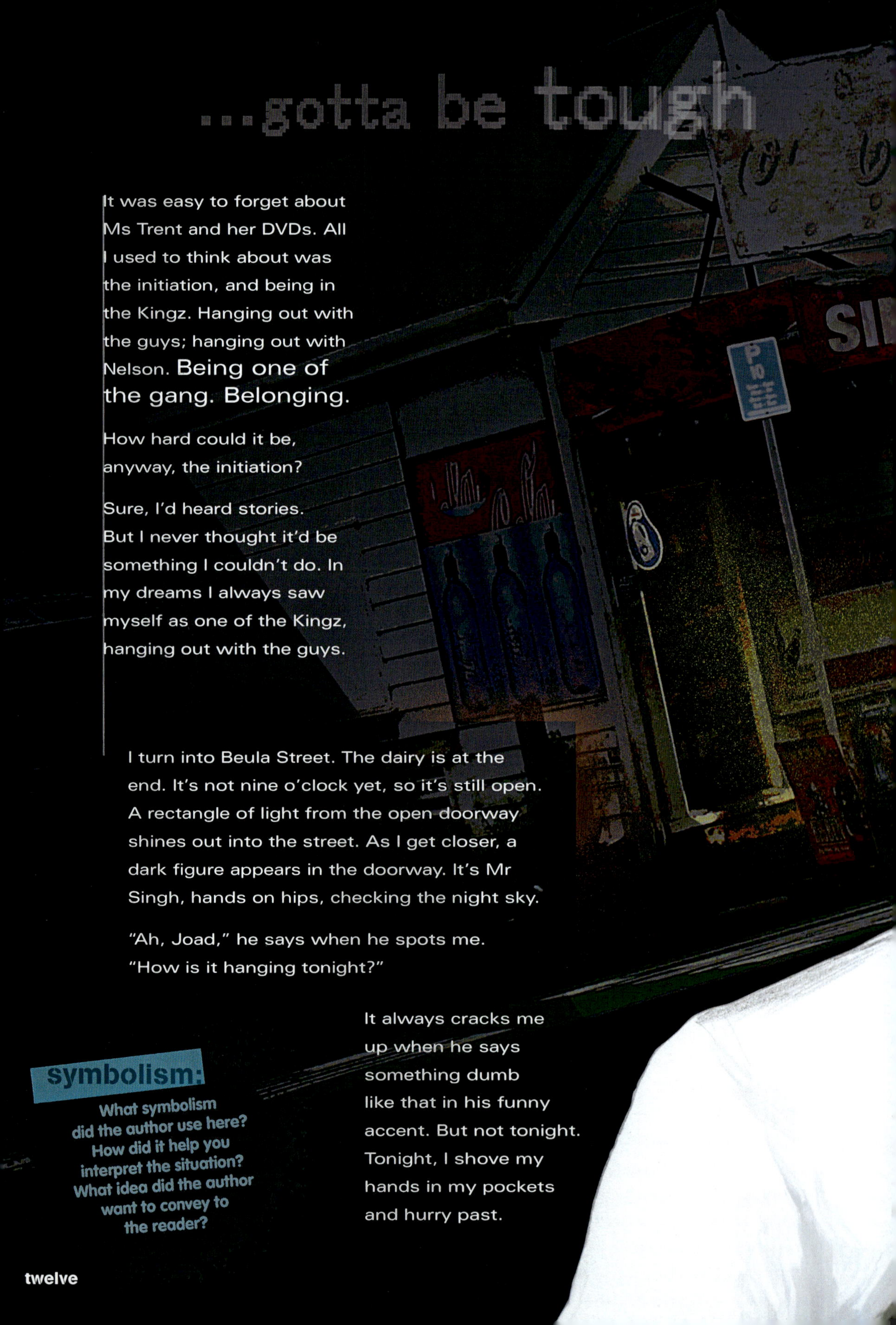

...gotta be tough

It was easy to forget about Ms Trent and her DVDs. All I used to think about was the initiation, and being in the Kingz. Hanging out with the guys; hanging out with Nelson. Being one of the gang. Belonging.

How hard could it be, anyway, the initiation?

Sure, I'd heard stories. But I never thought it'd be something I couldn't do. In my dreams I always saw myself as one of the Kingz, hanging out with the guys.

I turn into Beula Street. The dairy is at the end. It's not nine o'clock yet, so it's still open. A rectangle of light from the open doorway shines out into the street. As I get closer, a dark figure appears in the doorway. It's Mr Singh, hands on hips, checking the night sky.

"Ah, Joad," he says when he spots me. "How is it hanging tonight?"

It always cracks me up when he says something dumb like that in his funny accent. But not tonight. Tonight, I shove my hands in my pockets and hurry past.

symbolism:

What symbolism did the author use here? How did it help you interpret the situation? What idea did the author want to convey to the reader?

opinion: Do you think the author has stereotyped Mr Singh? Why/why not?

"Come over and see Savinda soon," he calls after me. "You know how he likes to see you."

I hurry past, through a pool of streetlight, then into darkness. There's an alleyway on my left and I turn into it, breaking into a run.

It's a dead end and I throw myself against a brick wall, breathing hard. Bile stings my throat, but I swallow it down. You've gotta be tough to be in the Kingz. You've gotta make the hard decisions. Kingz don't feel fear. Kingz only act. Even if that means going against a mate.

What's one mate, I'm thinking. Just another guy.

clarify: bile

issue: "What's one mate, I'm thinking. Just another guy." What issues do you have with going against a mate? Should mates ever be sacrificed? Why/why not? What qualities do you think a good mate should have?

SHOOTING CANS

Me and Savinda, shooting cans out at the old car park. Cans lined up along the concrete block wall. There was a supermarket on this spot once. Even some houses in the area. But it's all industrial now. And the old car park's just long grass and mouldy, dumped rubbish. Evenings, there's nobody around, so it's a good place for target practice.

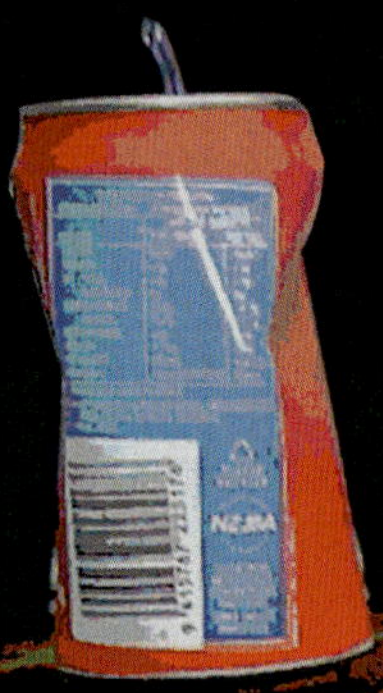

clarify: .20 calibre, souped-up

language feature:

ANALOGY

What analogy did the author use here? How did it help you to visualise the text? What did the author want to convey to the reader?

beyond the text:

Should people keep guns for protection? What are the **"for and against"** arguments on this?

...this is no toy gun

We use the handgun Savy's father bought a year ago when their shop got broken into. He lets Savinda use it whenever he likes.

A .20 calibre air pistol. For a guy in a wheelchair, Savinda's a pretty good shot.

Savy left school when he was fifteen so he could work in the shop, though he still liked to sleep late and play computer games all morning. So Mr Singh made him take the dairy money – the cash, the cheques – to the bank every morning. Savinda rackets along Beula Street like his wheels are on fire. It cracks me up. If it wasn't for the wheelchair, he might have been a boy racer in a souped-up car.

When he first showed me the air pistol, I didn't think much of it. "It'll just be like the .177," I said, thinking of the pistols in the city sports shop.

"Nah, man," said Savy, "this is no toy gun. Just wait till you hit some cans. You'll see."

Maybe I'm dumb, but it never occurred to me that other people would also know that Savy takes the dairy money over to the bank every day. I was wrong...wrong about a lot of things.

opinion: Do you think Joad has preconceived ideas about people in wheelchairs? Is there evidence in the text of prejudice? **Why/why not?**

Back home, Ma's eating salted peanuts and watching TV. She grins when she sees me and starts updating me about her favourite show. She watches it every night, never misses a single episode. I flop down on the couch, not saying a thing.

"Did they give you something to eat at work?" she asks. She doesn't know I wasn't working at the burger bar tonight. "I saved you some pizza."

But I'm not hungry. All I can think about is Savy and me shooting cans with his air pistol out in the empty lot, and what Nelson has told me to do.

"Joad," she says. "I'm talking to you."

The room feels too small. I want to hit somebody, smash something. I get out of there fast before I break something, like the TV. In the hall, I punch my fist into the wall. It doesn't make me feel any better, just hurts my knuckles.

author purpose:

Why do you think the author is still holding back information about the initiation test? What is the purpose of this?

inference:

"The room feels too small. I want to hit somebody, smash something."

What inferences can you make about what lies behind Joad's feelings?

clarify: updating

question:

Why does the author describe Nelson's eyes as black and empty?

character analysis:

How do you think Joad will measure up to the initiation? Use factual and inferential information about his character to form your opinion.

...he's been waiting

Next morning I go to school early, so I don't have to face Ma. My route usually takes me past the dairy. When Savy was still at school, I'd pick him up on the way and walk beside his chair as he scooted along. But today I go the long way round so I don't have to see Savinda or Mr Singh.

plot:
How credible/incredible is the plot so far? What predictions can you make about the resolution?

Outside the school, leaning against the wire fence, is Nelson.

"Hey," he says, and I know he's been waiting there for me. "You didn't say when you're gonna do the job."

The sky is metal-blue and I'm aware of other kids going past, looking at us, then looking away. Nelson's eyes are black and empty, but I meet his stare. "Tomorrow," I say. "I'll do the job tomorrow."

He nods, and walks away.

INITIATION

Ma had me when she was only sixteen. My father wasn't much older. I try and imagine what that would be like – to be a father so young. Just thinking about that makes it hard for me to breathe. Maybe that's why my father took off – he didn't want to grow up so fast. I asked Ma about it once, but she wouldn't say.

"Where did he go?" I asked her.

She just shrugged. "Somewhere down country."

He'll be thirty-two by now, and I don't know what he looks like. It's hard to imagine him being grown-up. In my mind, he's still a kid. We get a card each Christmas, so we know he's alive. And each Christmas, it's a different postmark.

analyse:

Is Joad's view of his father realistic? Why/why not?

I imagine my father working on a sheep station, riding a horse and rounding up the sheep. I imagine him working on a building site. I imagine him working on a fishing boat, hauling up oysters from the ocean floor. The one thing I can't imagine is him ever coming back.

And I think about Nelson again, waiting for me outside school.

More than anything, I want to join the Kingz. The initiation doesn't change a thing.

author purpose:

"The one thing I can't imagine is [Dad] ever coming back. And I think about Nelson again, waiting for me outside school." **Why do you think the author made the connection between Joad's dad never coming back and Nelson waiting at the school gate? What is the significance of this link?**

...wanting to make my mind blank

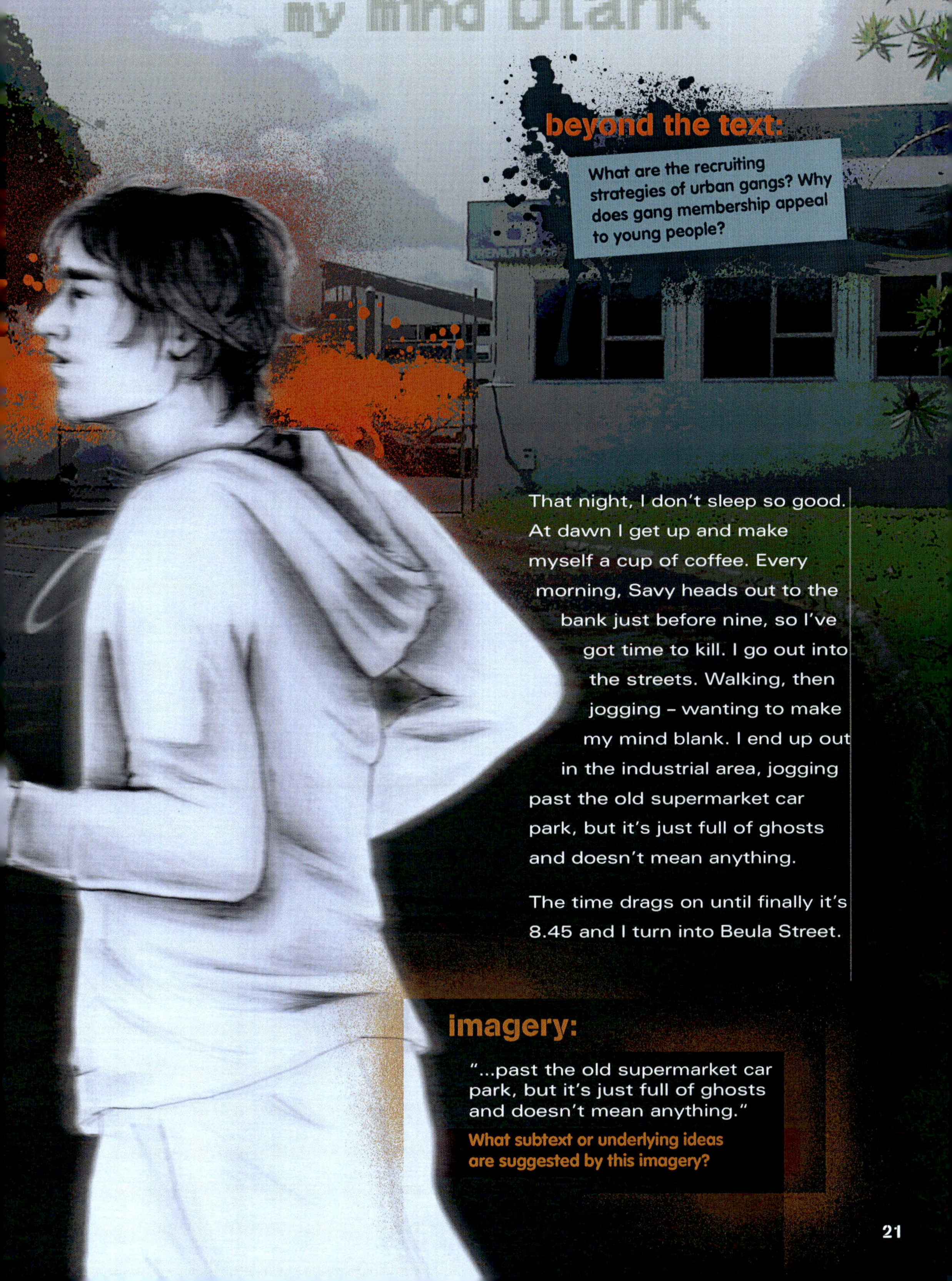

beyond the text:

What are the recruiting strategies of urban gangs? Why does gang membership appeal to young people?

That night, I don't sleep so good. At dawn I get up and make myself a cup of coffee. Every morning, Savy heads out to the bank just before nine, so I've got time to kill. I go out into the streets. Walking, then jogging – wanting to make my mind blank. I end up out in the industrial area, jogging past the old supermarket car park, but it's just full of ghosts and doesn't mean anything.

The time drags on until finally it's 8.45 and I turn into Beula Street.

imagery:

"...past the old supermarket car park, but it's just full of ghosts and doesn't mean anything."

What subtext or underlying ideas are suggested by this imagery?

beyond the text:

What consequences should Joad face for his actions in today's justice system?

clarify: running like a crim

personal response:

What personal feelings were evoked by the actions of Joad as he holds up his old friend Savinda?

Savy's coming out of the dairy, his chair running down the wooden ramp and out onto the pavement, his hands pedalling hard at the wheels. He's headed the other way, fast, and hasn't seen me. I break into a jog. Past the dairy. Checking the street as I jog – nobody about. A car flashes past.

I catch him up – Indian guy in a wheelchair.

"Hey, Joad." He grins, slowing.

Then his face changes. He can see it in my eyes, what I'm gonna do. For a split second, that thought passes between us. Then I make a grab for the backpack on his lap. But Savinda's got hold of it.

"Joad –"

I'm pulling at the pack, but he's hanging on tight. His muscles are tough from all that pedalling.

The gun's tucked in down the side of the chair. It only takes a second – I grab the gun and wave it around. "Gimme the pack."

Savinda looks at me. He isn't scared. My hand, gripping the gun, is white. In that instant, I'm ready to pull the trigger. He keeps looking at me, then lets go of the pack. Next moment I'm running, the gun in my hand.

On the main street there are more people, so I shove the gun in my jacket pocket. Running like a crim. Along the street, through the doorway and up the stairs to our flat.

Panting hard, I slam shut the front door. I've done it – my initiation. Tonight, once it's dark, I'll take the pack down to the river and give it to Nelson. Maybe the gun, too.

...I've done it

reading between the lines:

What strategies did Joad use in order to follow through with the hold-up of Savinda in his wheelchair?

SINGHS' DAIRY

There's a noise. Ma is standing in the kitchen doorway, staring at me. Man, what's she doing here? She's supposed to be at work. Why isn't she at work? She's wiping her hands on a tea towel, and looking at the pack.

"What've you got there, Joad?"

I slam into my room, shoving the pack under the bed. But she follows me, pale as a ghost.

"Leave me alone," I shout.

"Not till you tell me what's in that pack," she says. And for a moment it's like she's shining a torch in my face. "I know that look," she says quietly. "I've seen it before...the day your father left the city." Her words hang like ice in the air.

inference:

What inference can you make about why Joad wants to avoid close contact with his mum as she questions him about the stolen backpack?

I want her to get out of my room, but different words come out instead: "What d'you mean?"

Ma sits on the bed. I shift over to the window, not wanting her near me. She shrugs and looks at the tea towel in her hands. "It was late. I hadn't seen him for two days."

My voice sounds cracked and hard in the small room. "Yeah, and?"

symbolism:

Why has the author introduced the reference to the torch shining into a face? What does this suggest to you? What does the torchlight stand for?

"The police came the next day, but your father was already gone." Ma looks up at me. There are tears in her eyes and I don't think she's even seeing me. "There'd been a robbery down at Singhs' dairy," she said. "Two kids who wanted cash. A gun was fired...I think by accident. It wouldn't have done any damage, except the bullet ricocheted off a metal shelf and hit the kiddie, who was just coming out to see his dad."

opinion:

Do you think Ma should have told Joad about his father's criminal past sooner? What justification could his mother have for withholding this information?

...all I can see is me...Savinda...

Everything slips sideways, like a jigsaw puzzle falling off the edge of a table.

Savinda told me once how he'd been born crippled. We never talked about it again after that. It didn't seem to matter. Wasn't something we needed to talk about.

I hear Ma quietly leave the room, but I stay at the window, staring out. All I can see is me waving the gun at Savinda's head.

plot:

What impact did the twist in the plot have on you?

I'm standing across the street from the dairy, holding the pack. People go in and out of the dairy – buying newspapers, bread, milk, just like any other day. Savinda's mother or father will be inside, behind the counter. Savy will be out the back, in the part where they live. I've been out back there heaps of times – times when Mrs Singh has dished me up a plate of lentil stew, or poured out glasses of cola for us. Maybe Savy will be at the kitchen table, surfing the Net on his laptop or playing computer games.

I think about how my father took off that time, and how he's been on the run ever since. And I think about Nelson outside the DVD shop, pushing Ms Trent up against the wall. Hadn't realised till then how puny Nelson looks from a distance.

messages:

What messages does the author convey to the reader?

...something

My palms are sweaty, but this is something I've gotta do. Can't stay out here forever.

I sling the pack over my shoulder and cross the road.

question:
Is it possible for Joad to put things right between his family and the Singh family? Why/why not?

character analysis:
Evidence from the text | Inferential information

Summarise what you know about Joad, Nelson and Savinda, using evidence from the text and the inferences you have made.

I've gotta do

author purpose:
Why do you think the author wrote the story?

Think about the Text

Making Connections

What connections can you make to the characters, plot, setting and themes of *My Name Is Joad?*

Text to Text/Media

Talk about texts/media you have read, listened to or seen that have similar themes and compare the treatment of theme and the differing author styles.

Text to World

Talk about situations in the world that might connect to elements in the story.

Planning a Contemporary Fiction

Contemporary fiction incorporates many different genres, such as mystery, science fiction, adventure, narrative, recount...

1 Think about what **defines** contemporary fiction

Contemporary fiction connects the reader with the complex situations and events of contemporary society. It incorporates themes and contexts that are seen as:

A REFLECTION OF THE PAST A MIRROR OF THE PRESENT AN INDICATOR OF THE FUTURE.

2 Think about the **plot**

Decide on a plot that has an introduction, problems and a solution, and write them in the order of sequence.

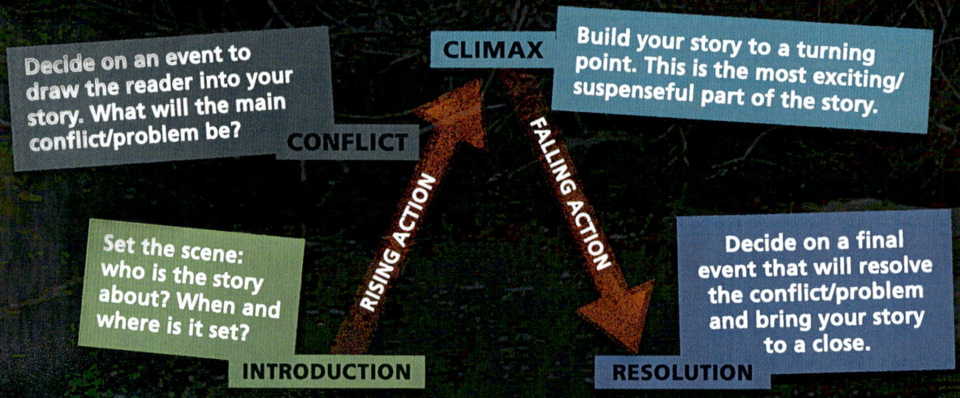

Think about the sequence of events and how to present them using contemporary fiction devices, such as *flashback* and *foreshadowing*.

Flashback – showing part of the storyline out of sequence.

Foreshadowing – suggesting or indicating events before they happen.

3 Think about the characters

Explore: how they think, feel and act

what motivates their behaviour

their inner feelings, using contemporary fiction approaches, such as stream of consciousness and product-of-society typecasting.

stream of consciousness – a description of the flow of thoughts and feelings through a character's mind as they arise

product-of-society typecasting – giving the characters roles that are typical of the society they were born into

4 Decide on the setting

atmosphere/ mood

location

time

Note: Contemporary fiction provides a window into current lifestyles and living conditions, which are often shaped by multimedia influences.

Writing a Contemporary Fiction

Have you...

- made links to the society and events of your period?
- identified with recurrent contemporary themes?
- maintained a fast pace of action?
- grabbed the readers' attention and dragged them from the first page to the final page?
- been true to the context of your time frame?
- provided a window on the past or present or future?
- explored contemporary values and beliefs?
- developed characters that will stand up to in-depth analysis?

...don't forget to revisit your writing.

Do you need to change, add or delete anything to improve your story?